BIG BRANDS

AMAZON

THE BUSINESS BEHIND THE "EVERYTHING" STORE

ADAM SUTHERLAND

Lerner Publications • Minneapolis

contents

the "everything" store

button will not display if:

- It is not available in your country of residence or location.
- Your device is not yet registered.

Menu: Tap to display a list of options. The menus are contextual, which means they change to offer appropriate options depending on what you're currently doing with the device. For example, on the Home screen of a Kindle with Special Offers, menu options may include Shop in Kindle Store, View Special Offers, Kindle FreeTime, Vocabulary Builder, Experimental Browser, Settings, List or Cover View, Create New Collection, and Sync and Check for Items. Note that you can view content on the Home screen using the default cover view or by list view.

When you're reading a book, menu

Loc 91   12%

The Kindle, with its huge library of digital content, has captured a new and rapidly growing market for Amazon.

What can you not buy on Amazon? From a sailor suit for your cat ($8.57) to a top-of-the-line Samsung 4K television ($3,267), Amazon stocks virtually anything and everything you can think of and will deliver it to your door in just a few hours.

In 2012, its seventeenth year of business, the company passed $61 billion in annual sales, employed more than one hundred thousand people (compared to Google's fifty thousand and Facebook's seven thousand), and is on course to be the first retailer to reach $100 billion in sales.

But, like many businesses, the road to Amazon's current success has been full of twists and turns. The company—founded by Jeff Bezos (pronounced Bay-zose)—started as a simple online bookseller that rode the first wave of dot-com enthusiasm in the late 1990s and grew to sell music, films, electronics, and toys.

Narrowly avoiding disaster following the dot-com bust of 2000 and 2001, it modernized its distribution network and diversified again into software, jewelry, clothes, sporting goods, and more. Then, having established itself as the Internet's top retailer, it extended its influence into technology with Amazon

Web Services' cloud computing and digital devices like the Kindle, Kindle Fire tablet, and now the Fire Phone.

Amazon is innovative and has changed the way the world views e-commerce. It's not the financial powerhouse of Google or even Facebook, however. Striving to put the customer first and offering everyday low prices means company profit margins are small, and the company was actually losing money as recently as 2012. But there is no doubt that Amazon has made and will continue to make a significant impact on the way we shop.

Business Matters
E-commerce

The Internet enables us to shop from our computers and even from our phones. Businesses can trade around the world without the need to open physical stores, leading to lower costs. Computer programs allow these businesses to learn lots of information about their customers and their buying habits.

Since 2010 Amazon has invested more than $14 billion to build fifty new warehouses, like this one outside Berlin, Germany.

the **birth** of the **business**

Jeff Bezos
Amazon founder

A gifted math and science student in high school, Bezos graduated from Princeton University in 1986 with a degree in electrical engineering and computer science. He worked in investment banking on New York's Wall Street before launching Amazon. His drive, ideas, and refusal to give anything less than his best have seen him named *Time* magazine's Person of the Year (1999) and Businessperson of the Year by *Fortune* (2012), as well as one of the richest people on the planet!

A mazon founder Jeff Bezos got a taste for the possibilities of the Internet while working for investment bankers D. E. Shaw & Co. in New York. David Shaw and Bezos often discussed the idea of an "everything" store—an Internet company that served as a middleman between customers and manufacturers and sold just about any type of product all around the world.

Bezos started to research the business and discovered that Internet activity was growing at a massive 230,000 percent each year! The young entrepreneur became convinced that he needed to launch a new business to take advantage of this opportunity.

Making a list of twenty possible product categories, he quickly decided on books for two main reasons: 1) there were just two main book distributors in the United States, so a new retailer would have to work with only two companies instead of thousands of individual publishers, and 2) at the time, there were three million books in print worldwide—far more than any brick-and-mortar bookstore could stock.

Amazon had a USP, or a unique selling proposition—its unlimited selection of titles. "With that huge diversity of [titles], you could build a store online that simply could not exist in any other way," Bezos said. "You could build a true superstore with exhaustive selection, and customers value selection."

Traditional book retailers, like this one in the Singapore Airport, can never offer the same wide choice as an online bookstore.

Bezos quickly put his plans into action, leaving D. E. Shaw & Co. to pursue his dreams. But where would he have his headquarters? Because US law stated that businesses did not have to collect sales tax in states where they did not have physical operations (for example, offices or warehouses), Bezos chose Seattle rather than heavily populated states such as California or New York.

In 1994 the company name Cadabra Inc. was registered, along with other domain names including Browse.com, Bookmall.com, and Relentless.com (try Relentless.com and see where it takes you today!).

Business Matters
The unique selling proposition (USP)

A USP is a unique quality about a company's product or service that will attract customers to use or buy it instead of a competitor's. As a "virtual bookstore," Amazon's USP was its huge range of titles that couldn't be found in any one physical store.

investing
in the future

Shel Kaphan
Amazon's first employee

A mathematics graduate from the University of California, computer programmer Kaphan met Jeff Bezos when the future Amazon CEO was still working at D. E. Shaw & Co. When Amazon was formed, Kaphan joined the new company as chief technology officer (CTO), building Amazon's first website from scratch and staying with the company until 1999.

B ezos knew he needed a more memorable company name and, searching through the dictionary, came across the word *Amazon*: the world's largest river. What better name for the world's largest bookstore? On November 1, 1994, Bezos registered the URL—and Amazon.com was born!

In Amazon's earliest days, Bezos funded the company with his own savings, putting in nearly $100,000 in the first two years. His parents invested another $100,000, even though Bezos told them there was a 70 percent chance they could lose it all!

The Amazon website launched on July 16, 1995—proudly proclaiming "One million titles, consistently low prices." It contained a virtual shopping basket, a simple search engine, and a secure credit card payment system. But that's where the similarities with today's site end. In the early days, when someone bought a book, a bell would ring on employees' computers, and everyone gathered around to see if they knew the buyer!

Amazon itself didn't carry any books, so it would order the book from a distributor, wait for delivery, and then ship it to the customer. Most books took a week to reach Amazon, and items that were harder to find took much longer, so the company was always struggling to stay on top of orders. The first week after launch, Amazon took $12,000 in orders and shipped just $846 worth of books.

The Amazon home page—more than just a bookstore

8

Business Matters

Company logo

Company logos are a graphic representation of a company's name, designed to be instantly recognizable. When Amazon first launched, its logo was a giant *A* on a blue background with a picture of a river snaking through it. Today's design combines the company's full name with an arrow running from *A* to *Z*. The curved arrow is also designed to look like a smile.

The vast Amazon River was the inspiration for Jeff Bezos's "everything" store.

Press coverage boosted brand awareness and therefore sales. By the start of 1996, revenues were growing 30 to 40 percent each month, but profit margins were slim. Amazon paid distributors 50 percent of the retail price but offered up to a 40 percent discount on best sellers. Amazon needed a huge amount of sales to truly fulfill its potential. But that meant putting even more pressure on a young company that was struggling to keep on top of ever-increasing demand.

Amazon goes public

As with many dot-coms, Amazon's rapid growth didn't mean immediate profits. In 1996 the company generated $15.7 million in sales but had a loss of $5.8 million.

More investment was urgently needed. A company in the Silicon Valley called Kleiner Perkins invested $8 million for a 13 percent share of the company. Amazon could now afford more staff, distribution centers, and computing power.

Bezos's new motto was "Get Big Fast." The bigger Amazon grew, he thought, the lower prices it could negotiate with book suppliers, and the more distribution capacity it could invest in to get books delivered faster and cheaper. The Amazon founder was in a race to be one of the biggest and best brands in the new digital marketplace because he believed it would also protect him from increased competition. "When you are small," he explained, "someone else [who] is bigger can always come along and take away what you have."

The drive to be bigger led to Amazon's IPO (initial public offering, where shares in a private company are sold on the stock exchange) in May 1997. The company raised $54 million, turning Bezos, his parents, and other early investors into multimillionaires overnight. More importantly, though, it provided more funds to invest in the company's continued growth and worldwide publicity that boosted annual revenues by a massive 900 percent per year.

When companies grow so fast, recruitment can be a problem—not just hiring enough staff to handle the growth but hiring the right people. To this day, recruitment at Amazon follows a pattern that Bezos learned while working for D. E. Shaw in New York. After an interview, everyone involved in the hiring process expresses one of four opinions: strong no-hire, inclined not to hire, inclined to hire, or strong hire. Just one negative view can fail a candidate. "Every time we hire someone," Bezos explained to colleagues, "he or she should raise the bar for the next hire, so that the overall talent pool is always improving."

The New York Stock Exchange hosted Amazon's successful IPO in 1997.

Business Matters
Initial public offering (IPO)

An IPO, or stock market launch, allows shares of stock in a company to be sold to investors, including the general public. The process transforms a private company into a public company and is mainly used by companies to raise funds to enable them to grow the business.

Rise in Value of Internet IPO Shares

Amazon.com
$1,000 in 1997 - **$239,045** today

eBay
$1,000 in 1998 - **$68,638** today

YAHOO!
$1,000 in 1996 - **$61,052** today

Google
$1,000 in 2004 - **$12,072** today

LinkedIn
$1,000 in 2011 - **$4,972** today

Facebook
$1,000 in 2012 - **$1,269** today

dot-com boom and bust

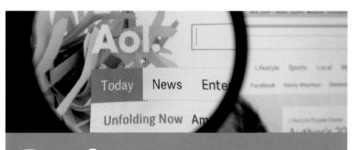

Business Matters
Profit and loss

A company's financial report, also known as a profit and loss statement, shows how the revenue (money received from the sale of products and services before expenses are taken out) is transformed into the net income (the result after all revenues and expenses have been calculated). It shows the revenues for a specific period and the cost and expenses charged against those revenues. The purpose of the report is to show company managers and investors whether the company made or lost money during a specific time period.

Books were never going to be Amazon's only focus. A key part of the company's early strategy was maximizing the Internet's ability to provide a better selection of products compared with traditional retail stores.

Management teams were charged with researching products with high SKUs (stock-keeping units, or the number of available items) that were underrepresented in physical stores and could be sent easily by mail. Early additions were CDs, DVDs, toys, and electronics.

Adding more product categories meant more warehouses were needed to house all the new stock. Between 1998 and 2000, Amazon raised an incredible $2.2 billion in further investment, opening five new distribution centers, recruiting new staff (the company grew from fifteen hundred employees in 1998 to seventy-six hundred at the start of 2000), financing deals with AOL, Yahoo, and other sites to be their exclusive online bookseller, and purchasing a number of existing online businesses—including Pets.com, Drugstore.com,

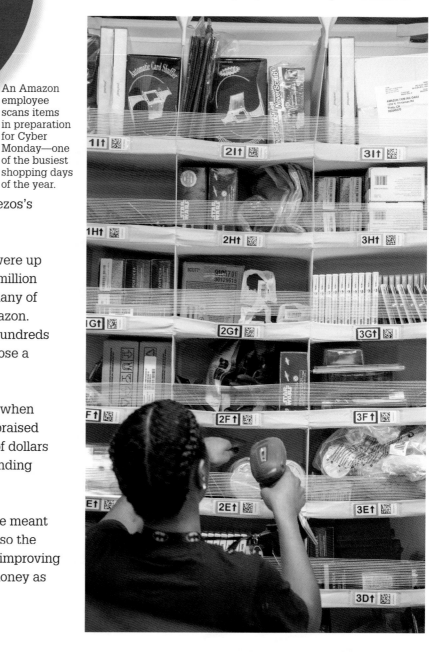

Tom Szkutak
Amazon chief financial officer (CFO)

Szkutak studied finance at Boston University before joining General Electric Co. He ran international finance operations for the company before joining Amazon in 2002. Szkutak, who retired in summer 2015, oversaw all Amazon's financial activities—keeping an eye on budgets, making sure the company was paying the correct taxes, and informing investors about the company's financial performance.

An Amazon employee scans items in preparation for Cyber Monday—one of the busiest shopping days of the year.

and Home-grocer.com—in efforts to achieve Bezos's ambition to be the "everything" store.

This ambition came at a cost. Although sales were up 95 percent in 1999, Amazon was left with $39 million in unsold toys after Christmas that year, and many of Bezos's acquisitions failed to thrive within Amazon. Most eventually closed, costing the company hundreds of millions of dollars. Amazon was on track to lose a massive $1 billion in 2000!

On top of this came the dot-com crash of 2000, when stock markets around the world radically reappraised the value of Internet companies with millions of dollars in turnover but no profits. Investors stopped lending money, and many companies went bust.

Fortunately for Amazon, a healthy bank balance meant there wasn't an urgent need for more funding, so the company could concentrate on reducing costs, improving its distribution network, and aiming to make money as soon as possible.

beating the competition

Establishing a successful company rarely happens without competition. In Amazon's case, it took on bookselling giant Barnes and Noble and won!

The long-established book chain had achieved $2 billion in sales in 1996, compared to Amazon's tiny $16 million but was nevertheless wary of the newcomer's growing appeal. The Barnes and Noble owners met with Bezos and his team to discuss a deal to buy Amazon. The offer was never made, however, and Barnes and Noble eventually decided to launch a rival website.

The corporate giants were very slow, allowing Amazon the time not only to expand its customer base but also to add important innovations to the site.

Bezos believed that if Amazon had more user-generated book reviews, it would have a huge advantage. Publishers complained when they saw bad reviews of their books, but Bezos stood firm. "We don't make money when we sell things," he explained to one publisher. "We make money when we help customers make purchase decisions."

Another idea that helped Amazon stand out was the idea of 1-Click ordering. Bezos told programmers he wanted to make it as easy as possible for customers to buy things on the site. So they devised a system that preloaded a customer's credit card details and a preferred shipping address and then offered the customer the chance to make a purchase with a single press of a button. Not only had Amazon simplified a buying process that could lead to millions more dollars in orders, but by filing a patent on the technology, it also prevented other companies from copying the process!

Building the Brand
First-mover advantage

Companies that enter a particular market—in Amazon's case, online bookselling—before any competitors can often gain important advantages. They have the opportunity to develop customer loyalty and brand recognition, get access to investment funding, and develop new technologies before their rivals.

Business Matters
Core values

The fundamental beliefs that guide a business are called its core values. They help a business set goals and decide on actions. Amazon's core values were defined by Bezos in 1998 and are these:
* Customer obsession
* Frugality
* Bias for action
* Ownership
* High bar for talent
* Innovation

Barnes and Noble reacted too slowly to the growth of online retailing, allowing Amazon to thrive with little competition.

the competitive edge

Toys "R" Us has used Amazon's distribution network to reach its own customers.

As early as 1997, Amazon was looking at the success of auction site eBay and trying to incorporate third-party sellers into Amazon, with commission from every sale helping to boost company profits.

> There are two kinds of retailers: there are those folks who work to figure how to charge more, and there are companies that work to figure how to charge less, and we are going to be the second, full stop.
>
> **Jeff Bezos**

In 2000 Bezos began telling colleagues that by the time Amazon reached $200 billion in sales, he expected revenue to be split equally between what Amazon sold itself and commission from other sellers using the site.

The same year, Amazon announced a deal with Toys "R" Us to be its exclusive online partner. The toy retailer would use its experience to choose the right toys for each season and negotiate low prices with manufacturers. Amazon would attract the maximum number of online customers and ship products on time. Similar deals followed with AOL's shopping channel, electronics retailer Circuit City, and even book chain Borders.

All these partnerships were short-lived, however, as Bezos's obsession with offering customers the lowest possible prices and the widest choice created tension with other retailers. Amazon Marketplace,

which launched in November 2000, raised protests from American publishers' and authors' organizations because the sales of used books affected the purchase of new ones and reduced author royalties (the money an author makes each time his or her book is sold). Even Amazon staff objected as Marketplace effectively meant they could lose sales to competition from within their own website!

Nevertheless, Bezos's plan worked. In 2002 sales from third-party sellers made up 33 percent of company revenues, marketing costs were reduced, international revenues were up, and Amazon finally made a profit—$5 million. In the first three months of 2003, Amazon achieved $1 billion in sales for the first time during a non-holiday period. Third-party sellers—of everything from books to kettles to televisions—continue to boost Amazon's revenue to this day.

Even fellow bookseller Borders used Amazon's superior logistics before its closure in 2011.

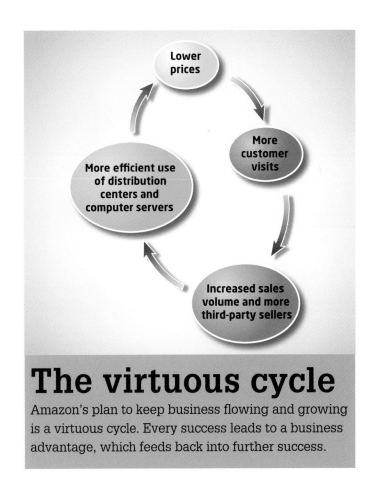

The virtuous cycle

Amazon's plan to keep business flowing and growing is a virtuous cycle. Every success leads to a business advantage, which feeds back into further success.

improving
the customer experience

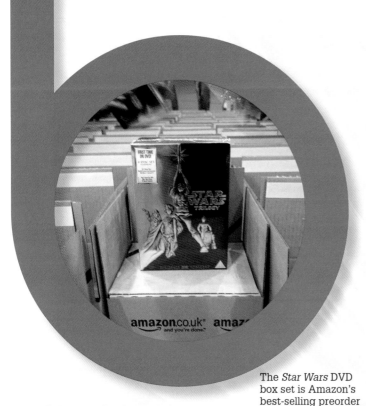

The *Star Wars* DVD box set is Amazon's best-selling preorder item ever!

Jeff Wilke
Amazon troubleshooter

Computer whiz kid Jeff Wilke has a bachelor's degree from Princeton and a master of business and science degree from the Massachusetts Institute of Technology (MIT). He joined Amazon in 1999, and his first job was making sure the correct orders went to the correct people as quickly and efficiently as possible. Wilke still works at Amazon, where he is the senior vice president of consumer business.

Amazon continued growing, expanding to nine thousand employees by the end of 2004. It also extended its worldwide reach—and increased sales—by launching a number of international sites, including www.amazon.cn (China), www.amazon.in (India), www.amazon.com.au (Australia), and www.amazon.com.br (Brazil).

Localized sites with more localized content is something that e-commerce is perfectly equipped to deliver, and Amazon used it as a way of expanding its customer base.

Another way of expanding the customer base, Bezos believed, was improving the customer experience. New features were added to the Amazon site, like "Search Inside the Book," which allows customers to search for words and phrases in a massive one hundred thousand books. Although publishers worried about online piracy, Bezos persevered, and when the feature launched, technology magazine *Wired* ran a feature on Amazon, praising the company for its innovation.

What better way of improving the customer experience than offering free postage? When surveys showed that shipping costs were one of the biggest hurdles to ordering online, Amazon decided

Jeff Bezos introduces the Kindle Fire in 2011. The tablet can be used to access Prime Instant Video—a video on-demand system to rival Netflix.

to offer free shipping for customers who were prepared to wait a few days for their purchases.

Eventually, Amazon Prime was introduced—a members' club with a ninety-nine dollar annual fee that enabled free next-day shipping. Prime was a gamble that could have cost Amazon millions in profits. Because the concept was untested, no one knew how many people would sign up or if Prime would positively affect customer orders.

The high cost of next-day delivery lost the company money at first, but it slowly achieved the goal of making customers "Amazon addicts," hooked on the almost instant reward of receiving purchases so quickly. Prime gradually boosted customer spending to more than cover its costs and has become a huge success—in fact, customers double their spending on the site on average when they become Prime members!

Business Matters
Diversification

Companies often decide to offer new products or services because it reduces the risk of its other products becoming too limited or boring. Amazon grew from being an online bookstore to selling music, DVDs, toys, electronics, fashion, and more. It became the "everything" store that Jeff Bezos had always wanted.

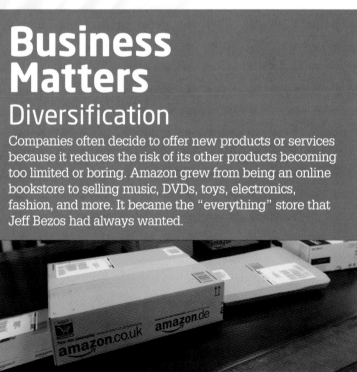

Amazon's headquarters, like the brand itself, is more functional and less space-age than Silicon Valley competitors such as Apple and Google.

Business Matters
Head-hunting

Companies often find suitable candidates for open positions through a process of head-hunting. Employees working in similar roles in other companies—often competitors—are approached and offered the chance for a new position. This usually includes an increase in salary and a promotion to a more important position.

life at Amazon HQ

The perks that dot-com employees often enjoy are legendary: free meals prepared by world-famous chefs, free transportation to and from work, and eye-poppingly futuristic offices. But Amazon is different. Aside from a bowl of dog biscuits by the front desk for employees who bring their pets to the office, Amazon expects its employees to pay for snacks and even office parking. The money the company saves, according to Bezos, is passed on to the customer in savings.

Occupying a dozen buildings south of Seattle's Lake Union, Amazon is also one of the few high-profile dot-com companies not based in California's Silicon Valley. Nevertheless, it still attracts some of the country's finest young thinkers, who often have to pass a baffling interview process. Bezos has been known to ask job candidates questions such as, "How many gas stations are in the United States?" He's not looking for the right answer—rather, he wants candidates to show creativity by coming up with clever ways to work out a possible solution.

Once hired, even the most technically brilliant Amazon employees are not allowed to use PowerPoint presentations to explain new products in team meetings. Instead, all staff write proposals, laying out their points in essay form because Bezos believes it develops critical thinking. The goal is to present a new initiative—from a new product line on the website to a new smartphone—in a clear, simple way that customers might read if they were hearing about it for the first time.

Bikes on Google's campus in Mountain View, California—a perk for employees

Bezos makes his e-mail address—jeff@amazon.com—available to all customers. He reads all the e-mails and forwards them to relevant executives with one addition—a question mark. Managers are expected to solve the problem and report back to Bezos within a few hours. If one customer has gone to the trouble of e-mailing him, Bezos believes, it's likely that hundreds if not thousands of others are experiencing the same problem. "Every anecdote from a customer matters," he says. "We treat them as precious sources of information."

> **There is so much stuff that has yet to be invented. There's so much new that's going to happen. People don't have any idea yet how impactful the Internet is going to be and that this is still Day 1 in such a big way.**
>
> **Jeff Bezos, plaque on the wall in Amazon's Seattle HQ**

never standing still

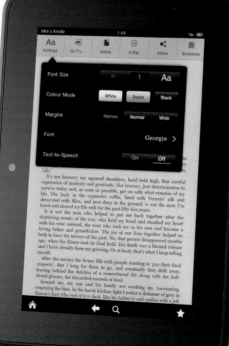

The Kindle Fire HD has helped Amazon break into the tablet market.

Between 2003 and 2005, Amazon lost many of its most talented engineers to Google, who had opened offices just twenty minutes from Amazon's HQ. The success of the Google search engine also put a barrier between Amazon and its customers. Because web users started their searches through Google rather than directly on Amazon, it meant that the site had to pay Google to advertise certain popular search terms like *flat-screen TV* or *Apple iPad.*

Bezos became convinced that he needed to transform Amazon from a simple online retailer to a technology company. "There's only one way out of this predicament," he told employees at the time, "and that is to invent our way out." Here are Amazon's main inventions since then:

Amazon Web Services (AWS)

Amazon's original cloud computing service sells storage, databases, and computing power to a range of businesses—large and small. Pinterest and Instagram rent space on Amazon's computers, and Netflix uses AWS to stream films to its customers. Even more important, the CIA and NASA use AWS's computing power to run their agencies. It's estimated that AWS generates around $2 billion in annual revenues.

> To me Amazon is a story of a brilliant founder who personally drove the vision. People forget that most people believed Amazon was doomed because it would not scale at a cost structure that would work. . . . But Jeff was very smart. He's a classic technical founder of a business, who understands every detail and cares about it more than anyone.

Eric Schmidt, former chairman of Google

The Kindle

The original Kindle e-book reader was released in November 2007 and sold out in just five and a half hours. Kindles allow customers to buy books, newspapers, and magazines from Amazon and download them through a form of Wi-Fi called Whispernet. In 2013 sales of the device reached twenty million, bringing in $3.9 billion in revenue, with an additional $300 to 500 million in e-book sales per year.

The Kindle Fire

Amazon's version of a tablet computer combines an e-book reader with a color screen to allow film viewing, with the functionality of a tablet for gaming and web surfing. The Kindle Fire launched in November 2011 in the United States and quickly became the second best-selling tablet on the market after Apple's iPad. Although sales figures have never been released, experts estimate around ten to eleven million Kindle Fires are sold every year—compared to roughly fifty million iPads sold annually.

The Fire Phone

This 3-D-enabled phone is Amazon's entry into the smartphone market. Released in July 2014, experts believe it has not been as commercially successful as the Kindle or Kindle Fire. Prices started at $200 for a 32GB version—a similar price to an iPhone 6 or Samsung Galaxy S6, and sales are believed to be less than forty thousand devices.

Amazon's 3-D-enabled Fire Phone has so far failed to make an impression on the smartphone market.

Business Matters
Fulfillment

E-commerce businesses have to master the process of fulfillment—registering customer orders, taking secure payment, and delivering goods quickly. Leading up to Christmas 2013, Amazon sold an amazing 426 items per second! An efficient fulfillment system was vital to ensure orders were delivered on time.

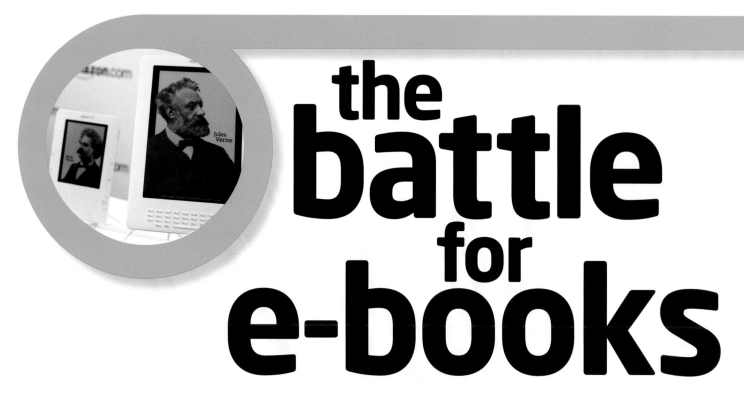

the battle for e-books

Following the launch of iTunes and the iPod, Apple leapfrogged Amazon and Walmart to become the top music retailer in the United States. With 74 percent of Amazon's 2004 revenues coming from books, music, and film, it was essential to Amazon's survival that it dominated the digital bookselling space in the same way that Apple did with music.

In the same year, Bezos announced to colleagues that Amazon was developing its own electronic reading device. It was a radical departure from the company's core retail skills, but Bezos believed that to succeed, Amazon needed to control the whole customer experience—combining well-designed hardware with an easy-to-use digital bookstore.

The goal was to have one hundred thousand titles, including 90 percent of the *New York Times* best sellers, available for download at launch. Immense pressure was put on book publishers to digitize not just new books but also many of their older products. As Amazon's importance as a bookseller grew, so did its economic power over publishers. Removing a book from its "recommended titles" list could cost a publisher up to 40 percent of its sales.

When Bezos introduced the Kindle in November 2007, he announced that Amazon would be selling e-books for just $9.99 each—undercutting publishers and taking a huge chunk out of their profits. Amazon quickly took a 90 percent share of the digital reading market, and five major US publishers—Penguin, Hachette, Macmillan, HarperCollins, and Simon and Schuster—tried to break Amazon's dominance by striking a deal to sell e-books through iTunes at mutually agreed prices, with Apple taking 30 percent commission on sales.

In turn, Amazon reported the publishers to the US Department of Justice for price fixing, and in April 2012, the courts ruled in Amazon's favor. Nevertheless, the argument over e-book pricing continues, and publishers are searching for ways to break Amazon's digital dominance over the market and reach out directly to book and e-book buyers.

The US Department of Justice announces an antitrust lawsuit against Apple in April 2012 for setting e-book prices too high.

Tom Hobbs and Symon Whitehorn

Kindle designers

British designers Tom Hobbs and Symon Whitehorn worked at design firm Pentagram and spent several years developing the first Kindle with direct input from Jeff Bezos. As part of their research, they studied how people turn pages and hold books in their hands. At Bezos's insistence, a keyboard was added to the first Kindle's design.

> "The Internet is disrupting every media industry. . . . People can complain about that, but complaining is not a strategy."
>
> **Jeff Bezos**

what does the future hold for Amazon?

Amazon is one of the world's most successful e-retailers, with $67.86 billion in revenues in 2013, compared to just $18.3 billion for its nearest competitor, Apple. So where does Amazon go from here? Jeff Bezos has already taken the brand from books to cell phones, so here are our predictions for Amazon's expansion in the next ten years:

For around $300 per year, AmazonFresh subscribers have access to all Amazon Prime services and same-day delivery on groceries.

Space exploration

Jeff Bezos's fascination with space goes back to high school. He has formed a new company, Blue Origin, devoted to space exploration and is "working to lower the cost of space flight to build a future where we humans can explore the solar system firsthand and in person." Amazon in space? We wouldn't bet against it!

Delivery by drone

Bezos introduced Amazon Prime Air on a US news channel, and the YouTube video has now been watched fifteen million times! This thirty-minute aerial delivery service by miniature flying robots won't be legal in the United States for a number of years, but as soon as it is, watch out for Amazon drones overhead.

Amazon groceries

Amazon's grocery service, AmazonFresh, has recently started up in California after a five-year trial in Seattle and is the company's attempt to grab a slice of the $1 trillion US food market. Revenues are slowly rising—a 23 percent increase for the second three months of 2014—so don't be surprised to see AmazonFresh deliveries across the country in the next few years.

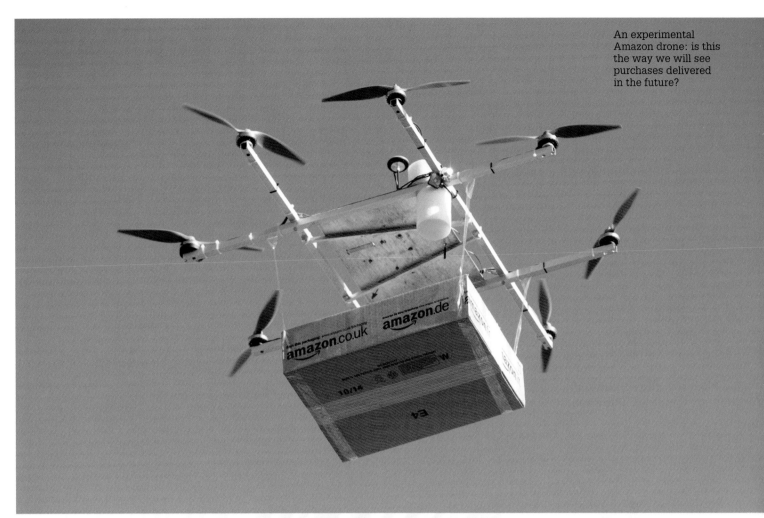

An experimental Amazon drone: is this the way we will see purchases delivered in the future?

> ❝ **This is Day 1 for the Internet. The alarm clock hasn't even gone off, and the world is asleep to what the rest of Day 1 will bring.** ❞

Jeff Bezos, the *Observer*, 2014

Amazon's facts

237,000,000
The number of Amazon customer accounts worldwide

$189
Estimated amount spent by each Amazon customer over a lifetime, compared to $39 on eBay

162,000,000
Unique monthly visitors to Amazon sites

10,000
The number of Olympic swimming pools that could fit inside Amazon warehouses worldwide

73.7 percent
Kindle's share of the e-reader market

market a new Amazon service

When a company launches a great new product or service, it needs to create a marketing strategy to sell it to prospective customers. Imagine you're launching a subscription-based selection of Amazon television channels. Here are the ten important steps you need to cover when writing your marketing plan:

Step 1: State your plan in a nutshell
Briefly outline what you will include in your full plan. This will be useful to give you and other readers a quick overview.

Step 2: Who are your target customers?
Describe the customers you're targeting—their ages, genders, interests, and what they want from a new TV channel or channels. Being able to clearly identify your target customers will help you pinpoint your advertising (leading to a higher "conversion rate") and also "speak the language" of possible customers. For example, a TV channel featuring romantic comedy films would be advertised differently from a channel featuring NFL games.

Step 3: What's your USP?
A strong USP helps you stand out from the competition. Amazon's USP is the "everything" store, but what would be the USP of its TV channels?

Step 4: Set your pricing and positioning strategies
Your pricing and positioning strategies go hand in hand. For example, if you want your company to be seen as a premium brand, then too low a price might make customers think that your product isn't top-quality. What are your competitors charging, and what do they offer for the price? In this section of your plan, outline the position you want in the market and how your pricing will support that position.

Step 5: What are you offering?

What special deals are you prepared to offer to attract customers to your service? Deals may include free monthly trials, money-back guarantees, or discount offers. Offering deals usually helps your customer base grow more rapidly.

Step 6: What's your promotion strategy?

This is one of the most important parts of your marketing plan, and it explains how you will reach new customers. Methods include TV advertising, online advertising, press releases, and so on—consider all the options and decide which ones will help you reach your target customers.

Step 7: What's your conversion strategy?

How do you turn prospective customers into paying customers? If you're using phone marketing, your "sales script" that the sales staff uses to persuade customers to subscribe is very important. If you're targeting possible customers by mail, testimonials—statements from existing clients who have tried and enjoyed the service—can be useful. Think about what would work best for you.

Step 8: Spread the word

If all your customers referred one new customer today, your service would double! To encourage customer referrals, prepare a referral strategy: Will you ask all your customers? How often? Will you offer a reward or discount?

Step 9: Keep customers happy

Many companies spend their time and energy attracting new customers instead of focusing on existing customers. If you're offering a subscription service like a TV channel, you need to keep existing customers and, ideally, entice them to spend extra money on one-time events. A monthly newsletter or customer loyalty program can increase revenues and profits by getting customers to purchase from you more frequently.

Step 10: How much money do you plan to make?

The final part of your marketing strategy is to make financial projections. Include the expenses you'll have and what the expected results will be in terms of new customers, sales, and profits. Also include the expected results from your plan to keep existing customers.

Your financial projections won't be 100 percent accurate, but you can use them to decide which promotions expenses will be the most cost-effective. Your projections will also set goals—for example, for your rates of keeping a consistent customer base—that you can strive to meet.

Completing a marketing strategy is hard work, but it's worth it. Stick to the plan, and your sales and profits should soar. Good luck!

glossary

anecdote
a short, sometimes funny story about something that someone has done

bias
a preference for something

cloud computing
the use of technology, services, or software on the Internet rather than software installed on your own computer

conversion rate
the number of sales of a product compared to the number of people who visit a website to look at that product

diversified
branched out to an array of different products or services to succeed in more markets or to protect against risk

dot-com
relating to companies that do most of their business on the Internet

entice
to persuade someone to do something by offering them a benefit

frugality
only spending as much money as necessary

innovative
using new ideas or methods

leapfrogged
to have improved a position by going past others quickly

maximizing
making something as big or as important as possible

middleman
a person or company that buys goods from the company that has produced them and makes a profit by selling them to a store or to a user

overview
a short description of something providing general information but no details

patent
the legal right to be the only person or company to make or sell a product for a particular number of years

perks
advantages, such as meals or a company car, that you are given for doing your job

pinpoint
to discover or describe the exact facts about something

proclaiming
announcing something publicly or officially

reappraised
to have examined a situation or activity again in order to make it more modern or effective

referral
the act of recommending to someone a product or service that you have personally used

retailer
a company that sells goods to the public, either in stores or on the Internet

royalties
payments made to writers, musicians, or other artists every time something they have created is used or bought by others

troubleshooter
a person who solves problems for a company

undercutting
selling goods or providing a service for a lower price than someone else

virtual
something that can be done or seen using computers or the Internet

further information

Books

Brandt, Richard L. *One Click: Jeff Bezos and the Rise of Amazon.com.* New York: Portfolio, 2011

Stone, Brad. *The Everything Store: Jeff Bezos and the Age of Amazon.* New York: Back Bay Books, 2014.

Web

Jeff Bezos, interview in technology magazine *Wired*
http://www.wired.com/2011/11/ff_bezos/all

Videos

Jeff Bezos, interviews on YouTube

https://www.youtube.com/watch?v=YlgkfOr_GLY

https://www.youtube.com/watch?v=pEZqCuEEMdU

index

First American edition published in 2016 by Lerner Publishing Group, Inc.
First published in 2015 by Wayland

Copyright © 2015 Wayland, a division of Hachette Children's Group, an Hachette UK company
published by arrangement with Wayland

Lerner Publications Company
A division of Lerner Publishing Group, Inc.
241 First Avenue North
Minneapolis, MN 55401 USA

For reading levels and more information, look up this title at www.lernerbooks.com.

Main body text set in Glypha LT Std. Typeface provided by Adobe Systems.

Library of Congress Cataloging-in-Publication Data

The Cataloging-in-Publication Data for *Amazon: The Business behind the "Everything" Store* is on file at the Library of Congress.

ISBN 978-1-5124-0588-0 (lib. bdg.)
ISBN 978-1-5124-0592-7 (EB pdf)

Manufactured in the United States of America
1 – VI – 12/31/15

Photo Acknowledgments
Cover: Ken Wolter/Shutterstock.com (top), Julie Clopper/Shutterstock.com (bottom); p1: Sipa Press/REX (top), DPA/PA (bottom); p4: Thinglass/Shutterstock.com; p5: PhotosJC/Shutterstock.com (top), John MacDougall/AFP/Getty Images (bottom); p6: EverettCollection/REX; p7: Tang Yan Song/Shutterstock.com; p8: Northfoto/Shutterstock.com; p9: 360b/Shutterstock.com (left), Janne Hamalainen/Shutterstock.com (right); p10: Natalie Fobes/CORBIS; p11: KPA/Zuma/REX; p12: Gil C/Shutterstock.com; p13: David Paul Morris/Bloomberg via Getty Images; p15: GilC/Shutterstock.com (top), mandritoiu/Shutterstock.com (bottom); p16: BarryBlackburn/Shutterstock.com; p17: Sipa Press/REX; p18: PA; p19: Sipa Press/REX, Sean Gallup/Getty Images; p20: Kevin P. Casey/Bloomberg via Getty Images; p21: Asif Islam/Shutterstock.com; p22: Liang Zou/Shutterstock.com (top), James Looker/Future Publishing via Getty Images (bottom); p23: Krisztian Bocsi/Bloomberg via Getty Images; p24: Andrew Harrer/Bloomberg via Getty Images; p25: Brendan Hoffman/Getty Images; p26: Kevork Djansezian/Getty Images; p27: DPA/PA; p28: irin-k/Shutterstock.com.